Collins

OCR GCSE 9-1
Design and Technology

Workbook

Paul Anderson and David Hills-Taylor

Contents

Manufacturing Processes and Techniques

Maths skills

Some of the exam questions for GCSE Design and Technology will use skills and knowledge that have been learned in maths. Some of the questions in this workbook require maths skills and they are labelled with this logo:

Exploring Context and Factors Affecting the Design Process

1 Designers must consider several factors when exploring the design context.

Give **seven** different considerations that designers should think about when exploring the design context.

1 ....

2 ....

3 ....

4 ....

5 ....

6 ....

7 ....   **[7]**

2 Explain **two** reasons why designers meet with clients to discuss the design context.

1 ....

....

....

....   **[2]**

2 ....

....

....

....   **[2]**

Total Marks .... / 11

Usability

1 Discuss the importance of using anthropometric data when designing products.

Use examples to support your answer.

....

....

....

....

....

....

....

....

....

....

....

....

....

....

....

....

....

....

....

....

.... [9]

Total Marks .... / 9

Exploring Existing Designs

1 Designers must consider several factors when exploring existing designs.

Give **seven** different considerations that designers should think about when exploring existing designs.

1 ....

....

2 ....

....

3 ....

....

4 ....

....

5 ....

....

6 ....

....

7 ....

....

.... [7]

2 State what is meant by life cycle assessment.

....

....

.... [1]

Total Marks .... / 8

New and Emerging Technologies

1 Give **one** example of a new and emerging technology that could have a positive impact on sustainability. Explain how it could do this.

New and emerging technology

Explanation

[3]

2 Give **one** example of a new and emerging technology that could have a positive impact on people's lifestyles. Explain how it could do this.

New and emerging technology

Explanation

[3]

Total Marks _____ / 6

Sources of Energy

1 The table shows different sources of energy.

Complete the table by stating whether each is renewable or non-renewable and describing how each is used to produce energy.

Source of Energy	Renewable or Non-Renewable	Description of How Energy is Produced
Nuclear fuel		
Solar energy		
Wind energy		

[9]

Total Marks _____ / 9

Wider Influences on Designing and Making

1 Explain **three** ways that a product can be designed to be more sustainable.

1 ....

....

....

2 ....

....

....

3 ....

....

....

.... [6]

2 What is meant by the term 'fair trade'?

....

....

....

....

.... [2]

3 State what is meant by ethical design.

....

.... [1]

Total Marks .... / 9

Viability of Design Solutions

1 What is meant by the viability of a product or system?

_____

_____

_____

_____
[2]

2 Discuss the factors that affect the commercial viability of a product.

_____

_____

_____

_____

_____

_____

_____

_____

_____

_____

_____

_____

_____

_____

_____

_____
[6]

Total Marks _____ / 8

Graphical Techniques 1

1 Produce a 3D sketch of a table suitable for use in a school classroom.

Annotate your sketch to show the materials and manufacturing processes that would be used to make the table. Explain why you have chosen them.

[5]

Total Marks _____ / 5

Graphical Techniques 2

1 a) State the purpose of a flow chart.

....

.... **[1]**

b) Explain **two** benefits of using a flow chart to plan the steps needed to manufacture a product.

1 ....

....

....

....

....

2 ....

....

....

....

.... **[4]**

2 Explain **two** reasons why a designer would create an exploded drawing of a design for a product.

1 ....

....

....

....

2 ....

....

....

.... **[4]**

Total Marks .... / 9

Approaches to Designing

1. The table shows three of the main approaches to designing.

   Complete the table by giving **one** advantage and **one** disadvantage of each design approach.

Design Approach	Advantage of Approach	Disadvantage of Approach
Iterative design		
User-centred design		
Systems thinking		

[6]

Properties of Materials

1 State the meaning of the following properties.

   a) Toughness

   ....

   ....

   .... [1]

   b) Electrical conductivity

   ....

   ....

   .... [1]

   c) Elasticity

   ....

   ....

   .... [1]

2 Name the material property described by each of the following statements.

   a) The ability of a material to resist being damaged by its environment

   .... [1]

   b) How strong the material is divided by its density

   .... [1]

   c) The ability of a material to draw in moisture, light or heat

   .... [1]

3 Explain the difference between a physical property and a mechanical property of a material.

   ....

   ....

   ....

   ....

   .... [2]

Total Marks .... / 8

Factors Influencing Material Selection

1 Explain what is meant by the following terms.

a) Functionality

....

.... [1]

b) Aesthetics

....

.... [1]

2 A designer has been asked to review the choice of materials for a product, to make it more environmentally friendly.

Explain the **environmental factors** the designer may consider when recommending an alternative material.

....

....

....

....

....

....

....

....

....

....

....

.... [6]

Total Marks .... / 8

Paper and Board

1 Explain the differences between carton board and bleached card.

_____

_____

_____

_____

_____

_____

[4]

2 A manufacturer has to cut as many copies as possible of the following shape from a piece of foam board.

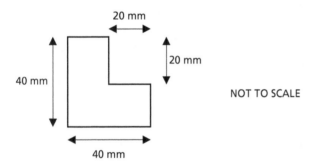

NOT TO SCALE

Sketching on the representation of the board provided, show how you would lay out the shapes to minimise waste.

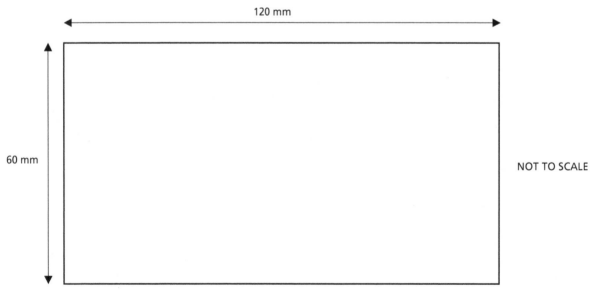

NOT TO SCALE

[2]

Total Marks _____ / 6

Timber

1 Using notes and sketches, explain how the differences between plywood and blockboard affect their properties.

[4]

2 Compare the **environmental impact** of using solid oak with that of using MDF to make furniture products.

[6]

Total Marks _____ / 10

Metals

1 Name the metallic elements that are the major components of the following metal alloys.

a) Stainless steel

....

.... [2]

b) Solder

....

.... [2]

c) Pewter

....

.... [2]

d) Brass

....

.... [2]

2 **a)** Name **four** stock forms in which metal is commonly available.

1 ....

2 ....

3 ....

4 .... [4]

b) Explain why a designer may modify a design so that a manufacturer can use metal in stock form.

....

....

....

....

....

.... [4]

Total Marks .... / 16

Polymers

1 Using notes and/or sketches, describe how thermoplastic polymers are produced from their raw materials.

[4]

2 A manufacturer is producing solid plastic cubes. Each cube is 30 mm on each side. The manufacturer is using a polymer with a density of 960 kg m^{-3}.

Calculate the mass of material needed to make 10 000 cubes. Assume that no material is wasted during the process.

[5]

Total Marks .... / 9

Textiles

1 **a)** Name a natural fibre that is used to make fabric.

.... [1]

b) Give a typical use for this fabric.

.... [1]

c) Explain why this fibre is an appropriate choice for this application.

....

....

....

....

.... [3]

2 **a)** Name a synthetic fibre that is used to make fabric.

....

.... [1]

b) Give a typical use for this fabric.

....

.... [1]

c) Explain why this fibre is an appropriate choice for this application.

....

....

....

....

.... [3]

Total Marks .... / 10

New Developments in Materials

1 Name a composite material and a typical application for which it is used.

   a) Material

   .... [1]

   b) Application

   ....

   .... [1]

2 Explain why superalloys are used in advanced aircraft engines.

   ....

   ....

   ....

   ....

   ....

   .... [3]

3 A company manufactures disposable knives and forks from polymers.

   Explain why they may prefer to use a biopolymer rather than a synthetic polymer.

   ....

   ....

   ....

   ....

   ....

   ....

   ....

   .... [4]

Total Marks .... / 9

Standard Components

1 Name **two** standard components that are used with each of the following materials.

a) Paper

1 ....

2 .... [2]

b) Fabric

1 ....

2 .... [2]

c) Metal

1 ....

2 .... [2]

d) Timber

1 ....

2 .... [2]

2 Explain why a company may decide to use standard components in a product.

....

....

....

....

....

....

....

.... [4]

Total Marks .... / 12

Finishing Materials

1. The table shows different types of material.

Complete the table by giving **two** finishing techniques that are suitable for use with each type of material.

Type of Material	Finishing Technique 1	Finishing Technique 2
Paper and board		
Timber		
Metal		
Polymer/plastic		
Fibres and fabrics		

[10]

Structural Integrity

1 A manufacturer is designing a casing for a hand-held torch similar to the one shown.

During testing they have found that the casing was bending out of shape when it was held by the user.

Explain how they could reduce the risk of the casing deforming.

....

....

....

....

.... **[4]**

2 Interfacing is a technique used in textiles.

   a) Explain the purpose of interfacing.

....

....

....

.... **[2]**

   b) Give an example of a textile product where interfacing in commonly used.

....

.... **[1]**

Total Marks .... / 7

Motion and Levers

1 State which type of motion is represented by each of the following descriptions.

a) Swinging backwards and forwards

.... [1]

b) Moving straight in one direction

.... [1]

c) Moving in a circle

.... [1]

d) Moving backwards and forwards

.... [1]

2 A first-class lever is being used to raise a load of 60 N. The effort needed to move the load is 24 N.

Calculate how far the load was applied from the fulcrum (length A).

....

....

....

....

.... [4]

Total Marks .... / 8

Mechanical Devices

1 Using notes and/or sketches, describe how the design of a cam can change the motion output from the follower in contact with it.

[4]

2 Two bevel gears similar to those shown are being used in a mechanical device.

The input gear has 48 teeth and rotates at a rate of 60 revolutions per minute (rpm).

If the output gear needs to rotate at a rate of 240 rpm, how many teeth does it need to have?

Not to scale

[4]

Total Marks .... / 8

Electronic Systems

1 The table shows different electronic components.

Complete the table by stating whether each component is an input or output device and giving an example application of each in a product.

Component	Input or Output	Application
Push switch		
Light-emitting diode (LED)		
Motor		
Light-dependent resistor (LDR)		
Buzzer		

[10]

Total Marks .... / 10

Programmable Components

1 A design is being produced for an outdoor security light system. A programmable component is to be used to control how the system works.

The programmable system must:

- Respond to a sensor detecting movement

- Turn on the light for a period of 10 seconds after the sensor has detected movement

- Turn off the light after the time period has ended.

Write a program that meets the needs of the security light system described above. You may use any programming language that you are familiar with.

[5]

Total Marks _____ / 5

Modelling Processes

1 Choose **one** modelling technique that you have studied.

Use notes and sketches to describe how you would produce a 3D model of a design using this technique.

Include details of all tools and equipment that you would use.

Modelling technique chosen:

[6]

Total Marks _____ / 6

Wastage

1. The table lists the tools and equipment used for wasting different materials.

   Complete the missing information. The first row has been completed as an example.

Material	Tool	Used for
Paper	Punch	Making holes
Wood	a) .... [1]	Making straight cuts by hand
Thin card	Compass cutters	b) .... [1]
c) .... [1]	Tin snips	Cutting thin sheet
d) .... [1]	Rotary trimmer	e) .... [1]
Textiles	f) .... [1]	Cutting a serrated edge to stop material fraying
Metal	g) .... [1]	Turning round parts

Total Marks .... / 7

Additive Manufacturing Processes

1 Describe the process of joining two metal parts using welding.

[6]

2 Explain how brazing is different to welding.

[4]

3 Name a metal joining technique that does not use heat.

[1]

Total Marks _____ / 11

Deforming and Reforming

1 Using notes and/or sketches, describe how a product is made using vacuum forming.

[10]

Total Marks _____ / 10

Ensuring Accuracy

1 Explain **one** reason why accuracy of manufacture is important.

....

....

.... [2]

2 Explain **one** example of how **each** of the following tools can be used to ensure accuracy of manufacture of a product or part.

Jig

....

....

....

....

....

Pattern

....

....

....

....

.... [4]

Total Marks .... / 6

Digital Design Tools

1 Give **two** examples of where a designer could use image creation and manipulation software as part of the design process.

1 ....

....

2 ....

.... [2]

2 Define the term 'digital manufacture'.

....

....

.... [1]

3 Define the term 'rapid prototyping'.

....

....

.... [1]

4 Explain **one** benefit of rapid prototyping products.

....

....

....

....

.... [2]

Total Marks .... / 6

Scales of Manufacture

1 a) State what is meant by batch manufacturing.

....

....

....

.... [2]

b) Give **two** examples of products that are made by batch manufacturing:

1 ....

2 .... [2]

2 Explain how moving to lean manufacturing can reduce costs in a manufacturing company.

....

....

....

....

....

....

....

....

.... [8]

Total Marks .... / 12

Large-Scale Processes: Paper, Timber and Metals

1 Using notes and/or sketches, describe how the process of offset lithography is carried out.

[5]

2 A manufacturer has an order from a customer for 10 identical cast parts.

Explain why the manufacturer might prefer to use sand casting rather than die casting for this task.

[4]

Total Marks _____ / 9

Large-Scale Processes: Polymers and Fabrics

1 Discuss the advantages and disadvantages of making a prototype of a product using a rapid prototyping process rather than by conventional machining processes.

....

....

....

....

....

....

....

....

....   **[4]**

2 Using notes and/or sketches, describe how extruded tubes are made from polymer.

[5]

Collins

GCSE Design & Technology

GCSE (9–1) Design and Technology

Principles of Design and Technology

Question Paper   Time allowed: 2 hours

You must have:

- the Insert.

You may use:

- a scientific calculator
- a ruler
- geometrical instruments.

Instructions

- Use black ink. Pencil may be used for diagrams and graphs only.
- Answer **all** the questions.
- The Insert will be found on pages 57–64. It must be used when answering the questions in **Section B**.
- Where appropriate, your answers should be supported with working. Marks may be given for a correct method even if the answer is incorrect.
- Write your answer to each question in the space provided. Additional paper may be used if necessary.

Information

- The total mark for this paper is **100**.
- The marks for each question are shown in brackets [ ].
- Quality of extended responses will be assessed in questions marked with an asterisk (*).

Name:

Section A

1 A pair of running shoes is shown in Fig. 1.

Fig. 1

(a) Explain **three** factors that should be considered when evaluating the design of the running shoes.

1 ....

....

....

.... [2]

2 ....

....

....

.... [2]

3 ....

....

....

.... [2]

(b) The running shoes are to be sold directly to consumers at a cost of £40. The cost of making one pair of running shoes is £25.

Calculate the percentage profit that will be made.

....

....

....

.... [2]

(c) Sketches of first ideas were produced during product design.

Explain **two** reasons why a designer would create 2D or 3D sketches of their initial ideas for a product.

1 ....

....

....

.... [2]

2 ....

....

....

.... [2]

(d) Explain **two** benefits of using sketch modelling as part of the design process.

1 ....

....

....

.... [2]

2 ....

....

....

.... [2]

2 A manufacturing company is planning to make a games controller similar to that shown in Fig. 2.

Fig. 2

(a) The casing of the controller will be made from a thermoplastic polymer.

    (i) Name a suitable thermoplastic polymer that could be used for the casing of the games controller.

    .... [1]

    (ii) Give **three** reasons why thermoplastic polymers are suitable for the casing.

    1 ....

    .... [1]

    2 ....

    .... [1]

    3 ....

    .... [1]

(iii) Describe the process of making thermoplastic polymer from its raw material.

....

....

....

....

.... [4]

(b) The company is using anthropometric data to design the controller.

Give **two** pieces of anthropometric data that the designer would need to know in order to design the games controller. For each, describe how it would influence the design.

Data needed 1:

.... [1]

How it would influence the design:

....

.... [1]

Data needed 2:

.... [1]

How it would influence the design:

....

.... [1]

(c) The manufacturer has carried out a survey of potential customers. They were asked which colour they would prefer for the controller. The results are shown in Table 1.

Table 1

Colour	Preferred by (number)
Black	12
White	7
Yellow	5
Silver	5
Gold	9
No preference	6

(i) Use the information in Table 1 to create a bar chart showing the number of people who preferred each colour.

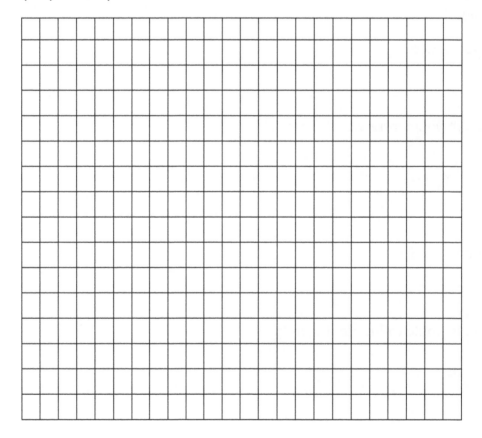

[4]

(ii) Calculate the percentage of people who had no preference for the colour.

[2]

(iii) Calculate the proportion of people who preferred black. Your answer should be expressed as a fraction.

[2]

(d) The company has calculated that each casing will contain 80 g of polymer.

It estimates that the process will produce waste of 2.5%.

Calculate the amount of material it should order to make a trial quantity of 6000 casings.

[3]

Practice Exam Paper

3   A designer has been tasked with designing a mobile phone charger that can be used when out camping.

Fig. 3 shows a mobile phone with a charger cable attached.

Fig. 3

(a) The designer is considering using solar panels to provide power for the product.

Circle the type of energy that solar panels provide.

Renewable   Non-renewable   [1]

(b) Give **two** advantages and **one** disadvantage of using solar panels to provide power for the product.

Advantage 1

....

....   [1]

Advantage 2

....

....   [1]

Disadvantage

....

....   [1]

(c) Give **two** ways of storing the energy collected by the solar panels.

1 .... [1]

2 .... [1]

(d) One of the solar panels will provide 900 milliamps of current. Convert this current value into amps.

....

....

....

.... [2]

(e) The designer wants the product to make a sound when the phone charging is complete.

Name **two** suitable electronic components that could be used for this purpose.

1 .... [1]

2 .... [1]

(f) Name **two** approaches that could be used to design the product. For each, explain **one** benefit of using it.

Design approach 1

.... [1]

Benefit

....

....

....

.... [2]

Design approach 2

.... [1]

Benefit

....

....

....

....

.... [2]

Section B

For all questions in Section B you must refer to the Insert. This contains images and information about products that you would find at an airport.

4   Refer to page 64 of the Insert.

    (a)   The person in **Image A** is wearing a jacket made from natural fibres.

        Give **three** reasons why natural fibres are suitable for this jacket.

        1 .... [1]

        2 .... [1]

        3 .... [1]

    (b)   The person in **Image B** is wearing ear protection that uses foam to cover the ears.

        Explain **two** reasons why foam is a suitable material for this application.

        1 ....

        ....

        .... [2]

        2 ....

        ....

        .... [2]

(c) The person in **Image C** is pulling a suitcase on wheels.

(i) Name the type of motion that wheels produce.

.... [1]

(ii) Name **one** electronic output device that could make the wheels on the suitcase move automatically.

.... [1]

(d) **Image D** shows a passenger jet aircraft made using composite materials.

Explain **two** reasons why composite materials are replacing aluminium alloys in aircraft.

1 ....

....

.... [2]

2 ....

....

.... [2]

You need to answer **questions 5 and 6** in relation to **one** of the products listed below covering an area you have studied in depth.

Information about the products is contained in the Insert.

Before you choose a product, read all parts of questions 5 and 6.

You **must** tick **one** box below to indicate your chosen product.

☐ Product 1: Gift Bag (Papers and Boards)

☐ Product 2: Pilots' Shirt (Fibres and Fabrics)

☐ Product 3: Automatic Car Park Barrier (Design Engineering)

☐ Product 4: Disposable Cup (Polymers)

☐ Product 5: Recycle Bin (Metals)

☐ Product 6: Café Chair (Timbers)

5   Study the images and technical information shown about your chosen product on the Insert.

(a)   Describe in detail how you would manufacture a **final prototype** of your chosen product in a school workshop.

Marks will be awarded for details of:

- The specific materials, components and manufacturing processes used to make the prototype.
- All tools and equipment used to both manufacture the product and ensure accuracy.
- The finishing techniques used.

[12]

(b) (i) Give **one** design method that ensures each different version of a prototype is evaluated and refined.

.... [1]

(ii) Explain **two** reasons why designers make prototypes.

1 ....

....

.... [2]

2 ....

....

.... [2]

(c)* Discuss the importance of considering usability when designing products for use in an airport environment.

Use the Insert to help you.

....

....

....

....

....

....

....

....

....

[9]

6 Use the same product you chose for Question 5 to answer this question.

It is important to consider the environment when selecting materials to use in products.

- Select a suitable material for your product based on its sustainability.
- Explain how this material choice would impact on the sustainability of the product.

Material chosen

Explanation

[6]

Collins

GCSE Design & Technology

GCSE (9–1) Design and Technology

Principles of Design and Technology

Insert

Time allowed: 2 hours

You must have:

- the Question Paper.

Information for Candidates

- This document is to be used when answering **Section B**.
- The images on page 64 are required to answer questions 4 and 5(c).
- The product information on pages 57–63 is required to answer questions 5 and 6.
- The question paper tells you when to refer to the information contained in this Insert.

Name:

Front view

Side view

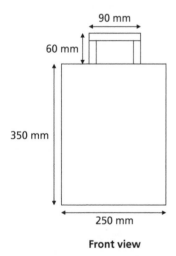

Front view

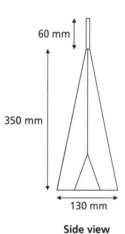

Side view

The bag is going to be batch produced. You need to consider the following needs for making the final prototype:

- How the design is laid out as a flat sheet prior to being made into a final bag.
- How the flat sheet is made into the final bag.
- How the bag that has been designed can be made so that it is recyclable.

Product 2: Pilots' Shirt (Fibres and Fabrics)

Front view   Back view   Side view

- The shoulder rank insignia patch is 90 mm × 40 mm.
- The shirt is to be made in the sizes shown in the table below.
- The final prototype of the shirt should be made to a large size.
- The shirt will be fastened using buttons.

	Extra Large	Large	Medium	Small
Neck to hip	690 mm	685 mm	675 mm	670 mm
Sleeve length	200 mm	200 Shim	190 mm	190 mm
Chest size	1220 mm	1120 mm	1020 mm	920 mm
Neck size	440 mm	430 mm	420 mm	410 mm

Product 3: Automatic Car Park Barrier (Design Engineering)

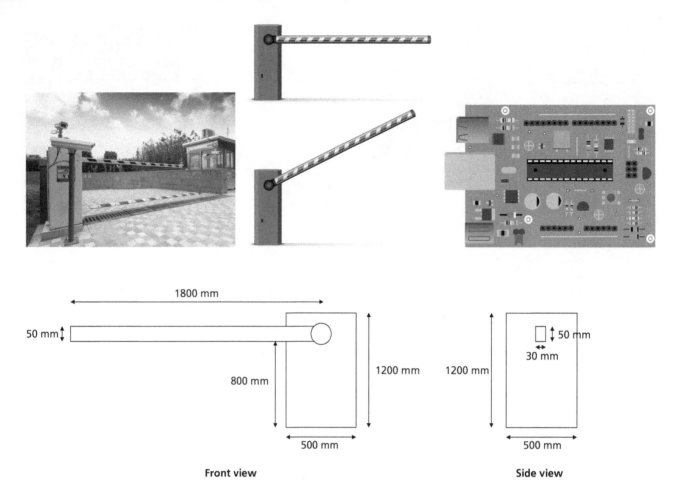

Front view   **Side view**

A car park barrier can be used to control access to the airport's car parking facilities. When a vehicle is detected at the barrier, the barrier opens. The barrier closes two seconds after the vehicle has passed through. This is controlled using a programmable device.

The final prototype should demonstrate to a stakeholder how the barrier functions. To do this you will need to use bought-in components, including a programmable device to control the opening and closing of the barrier. The prototype can be made as a scale model.

Product 4: Disposable Cup (Polymers)

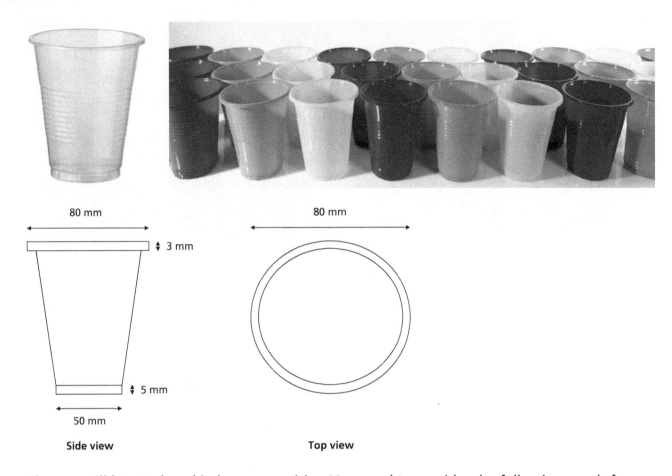

80 mm

3 mm

80 mm

5 mm

50 mm

Side view

Top view

The cup will be produced in large quantities. You need to consider the following needs for making the final prototype:

- The cup only needs to hold cold liquid. It does not need to hold hot liquid.
- Several cups should be stackable.
- The cup could be made in one of a range of different colours.

Product 5: Recycle Bin (Metals)

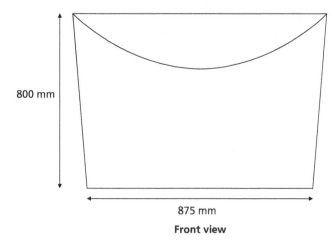

800 mm

875 mm

Front view

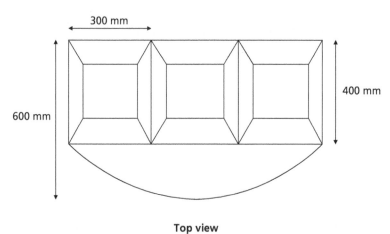

300 mm

400 mm

600 mm

Top view

Each bin will be produced using the same processes. It is designed to encourage greater recycling of waste in the airport departure terminal.

- The bin must be durable as it will be in constant use.
- It has three separate sections for inserting different types of waste: papers, plastics and general waste.

Product 6: Café Chair (Timbers)

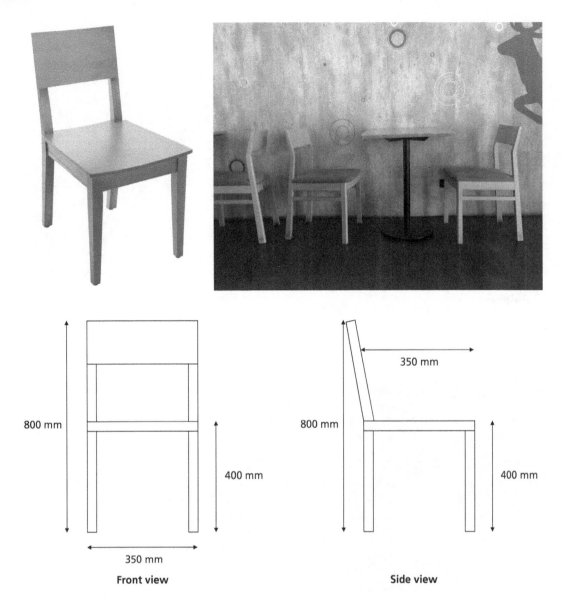

800 mm

400 mm

350 mm

Front view

800 mm

350 mm

400 mm

Side view

There are several chairs of the same shape, size and design used in cafés throughout the departure lounge of the airport. Some are cushioned for extra comfort.

- The chair is made from standard stock material. This is then cut and shaped.
- Suitable joining methods are used to attach the different sections of the chair together.
- The chair is strong but lightweight.

Practice Exam Paper Insert

Information on this page is required to answer questions 4 and 5(c).

Image A

Image B

Image C

Image D

Answers

Page 4 Exploring Context and Factors Affecting the Design Process

1. 1 mark for each suitable response. For example:
   - Where the product will be used [1]
   - How the product will be used [1]
   - User/stakeholder requirements [1]
   - Social factors [1]
   - Economic factors [1]
   - Social factors [1]
   - Moral factors [1]
2. Up to 2 marks for explanation of each reason. For example: to discuss the client's requirements [1] to ensure that they are considered during the design process [1]. To share initial thoughts about potential solutions [1] so that feedback can be gathered [1].

Page 5 Usability

1. 7–9 marks: thorough knowledge and understanding of the importance of using anthropometric data when designing products. Balanced discussion that comes to an appropriate, qualified conclusion. Several relevant examples presented to support answer. 4–6 marks: good knowledge and understanding of importance of using anthropometric data when designing products. Some balance to the discussion. Conclusion made but may not be qualified. Some relevant examples presented to support answer. 1–3 marks: limited knowledge or understanding. Mainly descriptive response and lack of balance. No conclusion. Few or no relevant examples presented to support answer.
   Indicative answer: Products need to be designed so that they are ergonomic. Anthropometric data is measurements taken from millions of people and placed in charts that can be used by designers to ensure products fit the human body and/or are easy to interact with. For example, when designing a chair the sitting heights should be considered when deciding how high the legs should be; shoulder breadth would determine the width of the chair. If anthropometric data is not used products may not fit the intended user. For example, if head circumferences are not considered when designing a hat, it may end up too big or too small for the user. The fifth to 95th percentile can be used to ensure 90% of the population are catered for.

Page 6 Exploring Existing Designs

1. 1 mark for each suitable response. For example:
   - Materials/components/processes that have been used [1]
   - Influence of trends/fashion/taste/style [1]
   - Influence of marketing/branding [1]
   - The impact on society [1]
   - The impact on usability [1]
   - Impact on environment/sustainability [1]
   - Comparison to past designs [1]
2. Systematically evaluating the environmental aspects of a product or system [1].

Page 7 New and Emerging Technologies

1. 1 mark for any appropriate new and emerging technology and up to 2 marks for explanation. For example: bioplastics [1]. These could be used to replace plastic carrier bags [1], therefore reducing the amount of oil that needs to be sourced [1].
2. 1 mark for any appropriate new and emerging technology and up to 2 marks for explanation. For example: nanotechnology [1]. This could be used to improve healthcare [1] by improving the delivery of medicines within the body [1].

Page 8 Sources of Energy

1. 1 mark for stating whether each source of energy is renewable or non-renewable and up to 2 marks for suitable description of how each is used to produce energy. For example:

Source of Energy	Renewable or Non-Renewable	Description of How Energy is Produced
Nuclear fuel	Non-renewable [1]	A nuclear reactor creates steam [1] that is used to turn turbines [1]. *Reference must be made to nuclear reactor or nuclear reaction producing steam to gain 1 mark.*
Solar energy	Renewable [1]	Solar panels collect light from the sun [1] and convert it into an electric current [1].
Wind energy	Renewable [1]	The wind turns turbines [1] that then drive generators to produce electricity [1].

Page 9 Wider Influences on Designing and Making

1. Up to 2 marks for explanation of each way. For example: choose recyclable materials [1] so that less new material needs to be sourced [1]. Design for disassembly [1] so that materials/components can be reused [1]. Select a sustainable power supply [1] to reduce reliance on non-renewable energy [1].
2. Up to 2 marks for definition. For example: fair trade is a movement that works to help people in developing countries [1] to get a fair deal for the products that they produce [1].
3. Designing with regard to people's principles, beliefs and culture [1].

Page 10 Viability of Design Solutions

1. Up to 2 marks for definition. For example: the ability of a product to grow after initial sales [1] because of recommendations [1].
2. 5–6 marks: thorough knowledge and understanding of the factors that affect the commercial viability of a product. Balanced discussion. 3–4 marks: good knowledge and understanding of the factors that affect the commercial viability of a product. Some balance to the discussion. 1–2 marks: limited knowledge or understanding. Mainly descriptive response and lack of balance.
   Indicative answer: Commercial products must make a profit when sold. There must be a suitable target market for the product. This must be identified, often through market research or by analysing the success of products made by competitors. If there is no market for a product it will not sell well. Being first to market can have a hugely positive impact on sales/can result in the product becoming the market leader, whereas being last may mean the market has already become saturated. No amount of marketing will be able to sell a poor product that does not do its job, so the product must be of the required quality. The selling price will affect how well a product sells. This will be determined by the cost of production, including the quality of materials and components used.

Page 11 Graphical Techniques 1

1. 1 mark for a 3D sketch that shows a suitable design for the table.
   1 mark for suitable material(s) chosen and 1 mark for reason why. For example: ABS (acrylonitrile butadiene) [1] because it has good toughness [1].
   1 mark for suitable manufacturing process(s) chosen and 1 mark for suitable reason why. For example: injection moulding [1] as it produces a very strong product [1].

Page 12 Graphical Techniques 2

1. a) To show the order in which a series of commands or events are carried out [1].
   b) Up to 2 marks for explanation of each benefit. For example: it provides a clear representation of the steps needed to manufacture the product [1], making them easier to communicate to other people [1]. It shows the exact order of operations needed to manufacture the product [1], making it easier to ensure the right equipment is available at the right time [1].
2. Up to 2 marks for explanation of each reason. For example: to assist with manufacture/assembly [1] as it shows how all the parts will fit together [1]. To explain the details of the idea to a client [1] as it shows each individual part clearly [1].

Page 13 Approaches to Designing

1. 1 mark for each suitable response. For example:

Design Approach	Advantage of Approach	Disadvantage of Approach
Iterative design	Problems with the design can be discovered and dealt with earlier [1].	It can be time consuming if a lot of prototypes or iterations need to be produced [1].
User-centred design	The end user has a greater ownership of the final product [1].	The design could become too focused on one particular end user's requirements [1].
Systems thinking	It is easier to find errors or faults in the design [1].	It can lead to the use of components that are not necessary [1].

Page 14 Properties of Materials

1. a) The ability of a material not to break when a force is applied to it suddenly [1]
   b) The ability of electricity to pass through a material [1]

c) The ability of a material to return to its original shape when a force is removed [1]
2. a) Corrosion resistance [1]
   b) Strength to weight ratio [1]
   c) Absorbency [1]
3. A physical property is a measurable characteristic of the material itself [1] whereas a mechanical property is a reaction to some form of applied force [1].

Page 15 Factors Influencing Material Selection

1. a) How well the product carries out the task that it was designed to do [1]
   b) How an object appeals to the five senses [1]
2. Award marks as indicated, up to a maximum of 6 marks. Whether the material is renewable/naturally replenished within a short time/made from finite resources [1] Whether the environment is damaged to obtain/extract the material [1] The amount (and impact) of transportation needed for the material [1] The amount of waste created when using the material [1] What happens to the product at the end of its usable life [1]; whether it is incinerated/goes to landfill [1] or can be recycled [1] Any other relevant point [1].

Page 16 Paper and Board

1. Award up to 4 marks as follows: bleached card is made from pure bleached wood pulp [1] and is white all the way through [1]. Carton board has white surfaces with grey fibres in between [1] and costs less than bleached card [1]. It also has slightly less strength [1]. The available thicknesses of carton board are typically slightly greater than for bleached card [1].
2. Award 1 mark for an attempt to tessellate that is inefficient. Award 2 marks for effective tessellation. For example:

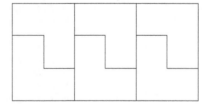

Page 17 Timber

1. Award up to 4 marks as follows, for information shown in either sketches or presented as notes: both are manufactured using layers of veneers positioned at 90° to each other [1]. In plywood these layers are through the full thickness of the material whereas in blockboard there is a central core of strips of timber [1]. This means the

properties of plywood are uniform in the x and y directions [1], whereas blockboard is stronger in the direction in which the strips are oriented [1].
2. Award marks as indicated, up to a maximum of 6 marks. Hardwood grows slowly, so cannot quickly be replaced [1]. It is cut from the tree as planks, which leaves a significant quantity of waste or unused material [1]. MDF can be made from either hardwood or softwood [1] and almost all the material is used/there is very little waste [1]. During its working life, oak is stronger and harder, so likely to last longer than MDF [1], reducing the need for replacement materials [1]. At the end of its usable life, MDF will normally either be incinerated or go to landfill [1], whereas oak could be incinerated (for fuel), but could also be broken down into particles to make MDF [1]. Any other relevant point [1].

Page 18 Metals

1. a) Award 1 mark each for iron and chromium.
   b) Award 1 mark each for tin and lead.
   c) Award 1 mark each for up to two of tin, copper and antimony.
   d) Award 1 mark each for copper and zinc.
2. a) Award 1 mark each for up to four of the following: sheet, plate, round bar, square bar, square tube and round tube.
   b) Award marks as indicated, up to a maximum of 4 marks: to reform metal it requires much energy [1] and effort [1], and therefore cost [1]. By using a stock form, this cost can be avoided [1].

Page 19 Polymers

1. Award marks as indicated up to a maximum of 4 marks, for notes or sketches communicating the following content: oil is extracted [1]; this is sent to an industrial refinery [1]; small chemical units called monomers are extracted from the oil [1], which are linked together to form the polymer chains in the polymerisation process [1]. This material can then be extruded/rolled/granulated into the required form [1].
2. Volume of 1 cube = 0.03^3 [1] = 2.7×10^{-5} m³ [1]
   Volume of 10 000 cubes = $2.7 \times 10^{-5} \times 10\ 000$ = 0.27 m³ [1]
   Mass of 10 000 cubes = 0.27×960 [1] = 259.2 kg [1]

Page 20 Textiles

1. a) Award 1 mark for cotton, wool or silk.
   b) Award 1 mark for a suitable application. For example: underwear, shirts and blouses,

T-shirts or jeans for cotton; jumpers, suits, dresses or carpets for wool; dresses, shirts or ties for silk.

c) Award 1 mark each for up to three properties that make it suitable for the stated application. For example: strong, durable and absorbent for cotton; warm, soft, absorbent and crease resistant for wool; smooth, lustrous and strong for silk.

2. a) Award 1 mark for polyamide/ nylon, polyester or acrylic.

b) Award 1 mark for a suitable application. For example: tights and stockings, sportswear, upholstery, carpets for nylon; sportswear for polyester; clothing, fake fur, furnishings for acrylic.

c) Award 1 mark each for up to three properties that make it suitable for the stated application. For example: strong, durable, warm and crease resistant for nylon; strong, durable, elastic and crease resistant for polyester; soft, warm and similar to wool for acrylic.

Page 21 New Developments in Materials

1. a) Award 1 mark for a named composite, for example glass-reinforced polyester (GRP), fibreglass, carbon-reinforced polyester (CRP) or reinforced concrete.

b) Award 1 mark for a suitable application for the composite stated in (a). For example: car bodies or boat hulls for GRP and fibreglass; tent poles or high-performance bicycles for CRP; buildings for reinforced concrete.

2. Superalloys are used in preference to other metals; they have excellent strength [1], corrosion resistance [1] and resistance to creep [1].

3. Award marks as indicated, up to a maximum of 4 marks: biopolymers are polymers produced by living organisms [1]. Synthetic polymers are made from fossil fuels such as oil [1], a finite resource [1]. Unlike synthetic polymers, biopolymers are biodegradable [1], carbon-neutral [1], renewable [1] and suitable to be composted [1].
Any other relevant point.

Page 22 Standard Components

1. a) Award 1 mark each for any two of: clips, fasteners, bindings.

b) Award 1 mark each for any two of: zips, buttons, press studs, velcro, decorative items.

c) Award 1 mark each for any two of: nuts and bolts, rivets, hinges.

d) Award 1 mark each for any two of: hinges, brackets, screws, nails.

2. Award marks as indicated, up to a maximum of 4 marks: making components in small quantities can be very expensive [1] due to the labour time [1] and equipment required [1]. It normally costs less to buy standard components [1] and more consistent quality can be offered [1].
Any other relevant point [1].

Page 23 Finishing Materials

1. 1 mark for each suitable finishing technique for each material. For example:

Type of Material	Finishing Technique 1	Finishing Technique 2
Paper and board	Laminating [1]	Embossing [1]
Timber	Varnishing [1]	Oiling [1]
Metal	Anodising [1]	Plating [1]
Polymer/ plastic	Polishing [1]	Self-finishing [1]
Fibres and fabrics	Brushing [1]	Bleaching [1]

Page 24 Structural Integrity

1. Award marks as indicated up to a maximum of 4 marks: use a stronger material [1]; increase the wall thickness [1]; add ribs to the outside [1] or add webbing to the inside of the casing [1], all of which increase the rigidity of the casing [1].

2. a) Interfacing means adding extra materials to a textile product [1] to increase its strength or make it more rigid [1].

b) 1 mark for a suitable example, for example shirt collars or behind button holes.

Page 25 Motion and Levers

1. a) Oscillating [1]
b) Linear [1]
c) Rotating [1]
d) Reciprocating [1]

2. Mechanical advantage = load / effort [1] = 60 / 24 = 2.5 [1]
For a first-class lever, as mechanical advantage = A / 60,
rearranging A = mechanical advantage × 60 [1] = 2.5 × 60 = 150 mm [1]

Page 26 Mechanical Devices

1. Award marks for notes or sketches communicating the following content. A follower can only rise (go up), dwell (be held at the same height) or fall (go down) [1]. How long the follower spends doing each of these depends on the shape of the cam [1]. A round section on the cam will provide a dwell [1]. The longer the round section, the longer the dwell [1]. A snail cam (or similar) will provide a sudden drop [1]. Any other relevant point [1].

2. Gear ratio needed = speed of output gear / speed of input gear [1] = 240 / 60 = 4:1 [1]
Number of teeth needed = number of teeth on input gear / gear ratio [1] = 48 / 4 = 12 [1]

Page 27 Electronic Systems

1. 1 mark for stating whether each component is an input or output and 1 mark for suitable application of each. For example:

Component	Input or Output	Application
Push switch	Input [1]	Starting the timing sequence on a kitchen timer [1]
Light-emitting diode (LED)	Output [1]	Providing light for a bicycle safety lamp [1]
Motor	Output [1]	Turning the blades on a handheld fan [1]
Light-dependent resistor (LDR)	Input [1]	Light sensor for a garden light that comes on when it is dark [1]
Buzzer	Output [1]	Making a buzzing sound for a doorbell [1]

Page 28 Programmable Components

1. 1 mark for showing how/where the program starts and ends, 1 mark for a way of checking the sensor, 1 mark for turning the light on after the sensor has detected movement, 1 mark for way of setting the correct time period, 1 mark for turning the light off.
Any appropriate programming language may be used, including raw code or block- or flow-chart-based approaches.

Page 29 Modelling Processes

1. 5–6 marks: detailed and thorough description of the technique. All tools and equipment needed are included. Detailed supporting sketches for every stage of the process. 3–4 marks: good description of the technique. Most tools and equipment needed are included. Some supporting sketches showing some detail. 1–2 marks: basic description of the technique. A few tools and equipment needed are included. A few basic supporting sketches.
For example, for producing a card model steps could include: Measure and mark out the card pieces required using a pencil, a ruler, a protractor, etc. Use scissors, a craft knife (with safety rule/protective mat) and/or a rotary trimmer to cut the card pieces to shape. Assemble the card pieces together using a glue gun, masking/ double-sided tape or other suitable tapes/adhesives.

Page 30 Wastage

1. a) Award 1 mark for tenon saw.
   b) Award 1 mark for cutting circles.
   c) Award 1 mark for metal.
   d) Award 1 mark for paper and card.
   e) Award 1 mark for cutting straight lines.
   f) Award 1 mark for pinking shears.
   g) Award 1 mark for centre lathe.

Page 31 Additive Manufacturing Processes

1. Award marks as indicated up to a maximum of 6 marks: the parts to be joined are cleaned [1] and any oxide, rust or grease is removed [1]. They are placed together to form the joint [1]. A heat source from a flame/electric arc is applied [1]. This melts the edges of the parts so they join together [1]. A filler wire may be used [1] especially if there is a gap between the parts being joined [1]. The joint is then allowed to cool [1] and cleaned/descaled if necessary [1].
2. Award marks as indicated up to a maximum of 4 marks. Brazing is carried out at a lower temperature than welding [1]. The parts to be joined do not melt [1]. A filler metal must be used: in welding this is sometimes not needed [1]. The joint is a different alloy to the parent metal [1]. A brazed joint is not normally as strong as a welded joint [1]. Any other relevant point [1].
3. Award one mark for either epoxy resin or riveting.

Page 32 Deforming and Reforming

1. Award marks as follows up to a maximum of 10 marks (information can be conveyed in either sketches or notes). A mould is made [1]. The mould is placed inside the vacuum-forming machine [1]. A sheet of material is clamped across the top [1]. The material must be a thermoplastic polymer [1]. The material is heated until it softens [1]. The mould is raised [1]. A vacuum is applied to suck out the air between the mould and the plastic [1]. Air pressure from the atmosphere pushes the plastic against the mould [1]. Air may be blown in to help the mould release from the product [1]. The mould is lowered and the plastic sheet is unclamped [1]. The product is cut out of the plastic sheet [1].

Page 33 Ensuring Accuracy

1. Up to 2 marks for explanation of reason. For example: a small deviation from dimensions given in the specification [1] can result in a product that is not fit for purpose [1].

2. Up to 2 marks for explanation of each example. For example: jig: holding and positioning a drill [1] to ensure that holes are drilled in the same place on two pieces of wood [1]. Pattern: providing a pattern for a dress [1] so that the parts can be traced accurately onto fabric [1].

Page 34 Digital Design Tools

1. 1 mark for each suitable response. For example: when preparing images of product prototypes for a presentation to stakeholders [1]. When designing a pictorial logo to go on product packaging [1].
2. 1 mark for correct definition. For example: approach to manufacturing that is centred around a computer system [1].
3. 1 mark for correct definition. For example: processes used to quickly produce a product or component directly from computer-aided design (CAD) data [1].
4. Up to 2 marks for explanation of benefit. For example: the prototype created can be fully evaluated [1] so errors in the design can be found before the final product is manufactured [1].

Page 35 Scales of Manufacture

1. a) Award marks as indicated: a group of identical products are made together [1], followed by other groups of similar (but not necessarily identical) products [1].
   b) Award 1 mark each for two suitable examples. For example: chairs, clothes for high-street stores.
2. Award marks as indicated up to a maximum of 8 marks. Lean manufacturing aims to eliminate waste during manufacturing [1]. Waste refers to any activity that does not add value to the product [1]. Eliminating waste normally reduces the cost required to make the product in some way [1]. There are many types of waste:
   - Time looking for tools [1], as this takes operator time which costs money [1]. This can be reduced by using tool boards [1].
   - Moving products around a factory [1]. This can be reduced by using conveyors/automation to move products [1] or reducing distances between processes [1].
   - Making too many products [1], as this ties up money in stock [1].
   - Doing more to the product than the customer needs [1], as this overprocessing [1] takes labour time [1] or can even involve buying more expensive machines than needed [1].
   - Making defective parts [1] due to the cost of material [1] and the labour cost spent on making the product being lost [1].
   - Any other relevant point [1].

Page 36 Large-Scale Processes: Paper, Timber and Metals

1. Award marks as follows up to a maximum of 5 marks (information can be conveyed in either sketches or notes):
   - The image to print is in relief on the printing plate [1].
   - Ink is applied, which is attracted to the image [1].
   - The plate is dampened, which repels ink of any non-image areas [1].
   - The printing plate transfers an inked image onto the rubber blanket cylinder [1].
   - The rubber blanket cylinder presses the image onto the paper or card as it is fed through [1].
2. Award marks as indicated up to a maximum of 4 marks: die casting uses a reusable metal mould [1] which is much more expensive than a mould made from sand [1]. Even though in sand casting a new mould has to be made every time [1], for a batch of 10 products the total cost will probably be less than the cost of the metal mould [1]. Further, the equipment cost for sand casting is much less than for die casting [1].

Page 37 Large-Scale Processes: Polymers and Fabrics

1. Award marks as indicated up to a maximum of 4 marks. A maximum of 2 marks can be achieved if only advantages or disadvantages are stated:
   - Advantage: rapid prototyping can produce a prototype much faster than conventional machining [1].
   - Advantage: the prototype can be produced directly from a CAD model [1].
   - Disadvantage: the mechanical properties of the rapid prototype may be different from the final product [1] as it may use different materials to those that the final product would be made from [1].
   - Disadvantage: the design may have features that cannot subsequently be manufactured using conventional processes [1].
   - Any other relevant point [1].
2. Award marks as follows up to a maximum of 5 marks (information can be conveyed in either sketches or notes). Plastic powder or granules are fed from a hopper into the machine [1]. Heaters melt the plastic [1]. A screw moves the plastic along towards the mould [1]. The screw provides pressure on the plastic turning it into a continuous stream [1]. The pressure forces the plastic through a die in the profile of the tube, creating the pipe [1].

Pages 38–48 Practice Exam Paper
Section A

1. (a) Up to 2 marks for explanation of each factor. For example:
   - The impact of current fashion/trends on the design [1], as a design that is not fashionable may not sell well [1].
   - Its potential impact on the environment [1] as a product that makes use of recyclable materials would be more sustainable [1].
   - How it compares to past designs [1] as customers would expect to see improvements from previous versions of the product [1].
   (b) Up to 2 marks for calculation. For example:
   £40 – £25 = £15 [1]
   15/40 = 0.375; 0.375 x 100 = 37.5% [1]
   (c) Up to 2 marks for explanation of each reason. For example:
   - It allows the ideas to be drawn quickly [1] as formal drawing standards do not need to be followed [1].
   - To keep the client focused on the general concept [1] as exact details do not need to be included [1].
   (d) Up to 2 marks for explanation of each benefit. For example:
   - It can convert hand drawings into 3D models [1], which saves time drawing them again in CAD software [1].
   - Any designer can use it with very little training [1] as it does not require specialist knowledge of using 3D modelling programs [1].

2. (a)(i) One from:
   - polypropylene (PP)
   - acrylonitrile butadiene styrene (ABS)
   - high-density polyethylene (HDPE)
   - low-density polyethylene (LDPE)
   - polyvinylchloride (PVC).
   (ii) Three from:
   - insulator
   - waterproof
   - tough/durable
   - lightweight
   - easy to mould
   - available in bright colours
   - easy to clean.
   (iii) Award up to four marks as indicated:
   - Oil is extracted by drilling [1].
   - This is sent to an industrial refinery [1].
   - Small chemical units called monomers are extracted from the oil [1].
   - These are linked together to form the polymer chains in the polymerisation process [1].
   - This material can then be extruded/rolled/granulated into the required form [1].

(b) Award marks as indicated. Two from:
   - Finger diameter [1] determines button size [1].
   - Thumb length [1] determines position of controls [1].
   - Grip diameter [1] determines diameter of held section [1].
   - Award credit for any other appropriate response.
   (c)(i) Award 1 mark each for correct selection of x (colour preference) and y (number of people) axes. Award 1 mark if at least one of the bars is at the correct value, and 2 marks if all the bars are the correct values.
   (ii) Total number of people = 40 [1]
   Percentage = 6/40 × 100/1 = 15% [1]
   (iii) 12/40 [1] = 3/10 [1]
   (d) Weight of polymer needed per casing including waste = 80 g × 1.025 [1] = 82 g [1]
   Total weight of polymer needed = 6000 × 82 g = 492 000 g = 492 kg [1]

3. (a) 1 mark for circling the word renewable.
   (b) Up to 2 marks for advantages and 1 mark for disadvantage. For example:
   - Advantages: solar panels have zero greenhouse/carbon emissions [1]; solar energy will not run out in our lifetime [1].
   - Disadvantage: solar panels cannot collect energy at night [1].
   (c) 1 mark for each suitable method up to a maximum of 2 marks, such as battery [1], fuel cell [1] or supercapacitor [1].
   (d) Up to 2 marks for conversion. For example:
   900/1000 [1] = 0.9 A [1]
   (e) 1 mark each for buzzer [1] and speaker [1].
   (f) 1 mark for each suitable approach. Up to 2 marks for explanation of each benefit. For example:
   - User-centred design [1]. There would be constant user feedback [1], which would result in a product that matches their needs better [1].
   - Systems approach [1]. This would provide a top-down overview of the system design [1], which would make it easier to explain to stakeholders [1].

Pages 49–56 Practice Exam Paper
Section B

4. (a) 1 mark for each suitable reason. For example:
   - They are comfortable to wear [1]
   - Easy to dye/good dye absorbency [1]
   - Good thermal properties [1].
   (b) Up to 2 marks for explanation of each reason. For example:

- It has good sound-deadening properties [1], which would protect the wearer from ear damage caused by loud aircraft engines [1].
- It is soft/flexible [1] and so would be comfortable to wear for long periods [1].
(c) 1 mark for each correct answer.
   (i) Rotary [1]
   (ii) Motor [1]
(d) Up to 2 marks for explanation of each reason. For example:
- Composites are more lightweight [1], which would reduce the amount fuel needed by the aircraft [1].
- Composites do not to corrode [1], resulting in less likelihood of crashes/accidents [1].

5. (a) 9–12 marks: information on the Insert has been fully analysed. Comprehensive and well-planned response containing an excellent description of the making process. Thorough knowledge of the appropriate materials, components, tools, equipment, processes and finishing techniques needed to make the prototype and ensure accuracy. Excellent use of specialist terminology. 5–8 marks: information on the Insert has been analysed adequately. Good response that shows some evidence of planning and contains a good description of the making process. Good and mainly appropriate knowledge of the appropriate materials, components, tools, equipment, processes and finishing techniques needed to make the prototype and ensure accuracy. Good use of specialist terminology, but some may not be appropriate. 1–4 marks: limited analysis of the information presented on the Insert. Limited response that shows a basic understanding of the making process. Basic knowledge of the appropriate materials, components, tools, equipment, processes and finishing techniques needed to make the prototype and ensure accuracy, some of which may be inappropriate. Limited and sometime inappropriate use of specialist terminology.
Indicative content; for example: for Product 4 (polymers):
- Materials: high-impact polystyrene (HIPS), polyethylene terephthalate (PET).
- Processes/techniques/skills: making moulds, vacuum forming, injection moulding or other appropriate forming/moulding techniques, rapid prototyping.
- Tools: saws/cutting tools, drills, files, vacuum former, injection moulding machine/injection press, 3D printer.

- Accuracy: jigs, moulds, templates.
- Finishing: using self-finishing polymers, smart colours/pigments.

(b) (i) 1 mark for iterative design [1].
   (ii) Up to 2 marks for explanation of each reason. For example: it allows stakeholders to evaluate the prototype [1], which results in improvements to the next iteration [1]. It helps with the identification of a unique selling point (USP) [1] which would make it more marketable [1].

(c) All responses should be in the context of an airport environment. 7–9 marks: thorough knowledge and understanding of the importance of considering usability when designing products for use in an airport environment. Balanced discussion that comes to an appropriate, qualified conclusion. 4–6 marks: good knowledge and understanding of the importance of considering usability when designing products for use in an airport environment. Some balance to the discussion. Conclusion made but may not be qualified. 1–3 marks: limited knowledge or understanding. Mainly descriptive response and lack of balance. No conclusion.
Indicative content:
- Inclusivity/ease of use: information text on displays of suitable size so that people with sight problems can see it.
- Information and desks (ticket collection, passport control, etc.) of height that can be accessed by people in wheelchairs.
- Suitable use of escalators, lifts, support vehicles, etc., for people who have difficulty getting up and down stairs, accessing the aircraft from the terminal building or moving long distances/moving luggage within the airport.
- Ergonomics/anthropometrics: use of anthropometric data for the design of products, such as leg length for chairs, finger/hand size for using buttons on car park ticket dispensers, etc. Use of ergonomics to ensure comfortable seating in terminal and on aircraft.
- Aesthetics: use of attractive and informative colour schemes on signage, use of calming colours/avoiding aggressive colours in terminal building to reduce stress.

6. 5–6 marks: thorough knowledge and understanding of how the material chosen would impact on the sustainability of the product. All points fully explained. 3–4 marks: good knowledge and understanding of how the material chosen would impact on the sustainability of the product. Majority of points explained. 1–2 marks: limited knowledge or understanding. Mainly descriptive response.
Indicative content; for example: for Product 4 (polymers):
- Use bioplastics instead of traditional oil-based plastics.
- This would result in less oil needing to be drilled for, thus reducing carbon emissions and reliance on fossil fuels.
- Bioplastics are biodegradable, thus reducing the amount of landfill waste produced.
- Traditional plastics can take thousands of years to degrade and cause damage and death to wildlife over a long period of time.

Rethink Revision

Have you ever taken part in a quiz and thought '*I know this*!', but, despite frantically racking your brain, you just couldn't come up with the answer?

It's very frustrating when this happens, but in a fun situation it doesn't really matter. However, in your GCSE exams, it will be essential that you can recall the relevant information quickly when you need to.

Most students think that revision is about making sure you **know** stuff. Of course, this is important, but it is also about becoming confident that you can **retain** that *stuff* over time and **recall** it quickly when needed.

Revision That Really Works

Experts have discovered that there are two techniques that help with all of these things and consistently produce better results in exams compared to other revision techniques.

Applying these techniques to your GCSE revision will ensure you get better results in your exams and will have all the relevant knowledge at your fingertips when you start studying for further qualifications, like AS and A Levels, or begin work.

It really isn't rocket science either – you simply need to:

- **test yourself** on each topic as many times as possible
- **leave a gap** between the test sessions.

It is most effective if you leave a good period of time between the test sessions, e.g. between a week and a month. The idea is that just as you start to forget the information, you force yourself to recall it again, keeping it fresh in your mind.

Three Essential Revision Tips

1. **Use Your Time Wisely**
   - Allow yourself plenty of time.
   - Try to start revising six months before your exams – it's more effective and less stressful.
   - Your revision time is precious so use it wisely – using the techniques described on this page will ensure you revise effectively and efficiently and get the best results.
   - Don't waste time re-reading the same information over and over again – it's time-consuming and not effective!

2. **Make a Plan**
   - Identify all the topics you need to revise.
   - Plan at least five sessions for each topic.
   - One hour should be ample time to test yourself on the key ideas for a topic.
   - Spread out the practice sessions for each topic – the optimum time to leave between each session is about one month but, if this isn't possible, just make the gaps as big as realistically possible.

3. **Test Yourself**
   - Methods for testing yourself include: quizzes, practice questions, flashcards, past papers, explaining a topic to someone else, etc.
   - Don't worry if you get an answer wrong – provided you check what the correct answer is, you are more likely to get the same or similar questions right in future!

Visit our website for more information about the benefits of these revision techniques and for further guidance on how to plan ahead and make them work for you.

www.collins.co.uk/collinsGCSErevision

Acknowledgements

The author and publisher are grateful to the copyright holders for permission to use quoted materials and images.

All images © Shutterstock.com

Every effort has been made to trace copyright holders and obtain their permission for the use of copyright material. The author and publisher will gladly receive information enabling them to rectify any error or omission in subsequent editions. All facts are correct at time of going to press.

Published by Collins
An imprint of HarperCollins*Publishers* Ltd
1 London Bridge Street
London SE1 9GF

© HarperCollins*Publishers* Limited 2020

1st Floor, Watermarque Building, Ringsend Road
Dublin 4, Ireland

ISBN 9780008326821

Content first published 2017
This edition published 2020

10 9 8 7 6 5 4 3

British Library Cataloguing in Publication Data.

A CIP record of this book is available from the British Library.

Authored by: Paul Anderson and David Hills-Taylor
Project management and editorial: Nik Prowse
Commissioning: Katherine Wilkinson and Katie Galloway
Cover Design: Sarah Duxbury and Kevin Robbins
Inside Concept Design: Sarah Duxbury and Paul Oates
Text Design and Layout: Jouve India Private Limited
Production: Lyndsey Rogers
Printed and bound in the UK using 100%
Renewable Electricity at CPI Group (UK) Ltd

MIX
Paper from
responsible source
FSC www.fsc.org   **FSC™ C007454**

This book is produced from independently certified FSC™ paper to ensure responsible forest management.

For more information visit:
www.harpercollins.co.uk/green